THE SHASTA

MICHAELA SEYMOUR

PowerKiDS press.

NEW YORK

Published in 2018 by The Rosen Publishing Group, Inc.
29 East 21st Street, New York, NY 10010

Editor: Theresa Morlock
Book Design: Michael Flynn
Interior Layout: Reann Nye

Photo Credits: Cover courtesy of UCLA, Fowler Museum of Cultural History; p. 5 Andrew Zarivny/Shutterstock; p. 6 Tom Reichner/Shutterstock.com; p. 7 rokopix/Shutterstock.com; p. 9 Auhustsinovich/Shutterstock.com; p. 10 Marilyn Angel Wynn/Nativestock/Getty Images; p. 11 jo M/Shutterstock.com; p. 13 Andriy Blokhin/Shutterstock.com; p. 15 https://commons.wikimedia.org/wiki/File:Hupa_Sweat_House.jpg; p. 17 ElaK/Shutterstock.com; p. 19 Lolostock/Shutterstock.com; p. 21 https://commons.wikimedia.org/wiki/File:Olivella_biplicata_3.jpg; p. 23 MPI/Archive Photos/Getty Images; p. 25 Courtesy of the Library of Congress; p. 27 Tony Moran/Shutterstock.com; p. 29 https://commons.wikimedia.org/wiki/File:Gullgraver_1850_California.jpg.

Library of Congress Cataloging-in-Publication Data

Names: Seymour, Michaela, author.
Title: The Shasta / Michaela Seymour.
Description: New York : PowerKids Press, [2018] | Series: Spotlight on the American Indians of California | Includes index.
Identifiers: LCCN 2017024782| ISBN 9781538324912 (library bound) | ISBN 9781508162896 (pbk.) | ISBN 9781508162940 (6 pack)
Subjects: LCSH: Shasta Indians--History--Juvenile literature. | Shasta Indians--Social life and customs--Juvenile literature. | Indians of North America--California--Siskiyou County--Juvenile literature. | Indians of North America--Oregon--Jackson County--Juvenile literature.
Classification: LCC E99.S33 S49 2018 | DDC 979.004/97--dc23
LC record available at https://lccn.loc.gov/2017024782

Manufactured in China

CPSIA Compliance Information: Batch #BW18PK For further information contact Rosen Publishing, New York, New York at 1-800-237-9932.

CONTENTS

WHO ARE THE SHASTA?. 4

LIVING OFF THE LAND 6

WHAT THEY ATE. 8

WHERE THEY LIVED 10

SOCIAL STRUCTURE. 14

GOVERNMENT. 16

RELIGION 18

TRADE 20

WARFARE. 22

SPANISH ARRIVAL 24

A CHANGING WORLD. 26

THE SHASTA AND THE UNITED STATES . .28

THE SHASTA TODAY 30

GLOSSARY 31

INDEX. 32

PRIMARY SOURCE LIST. 32

WEBSITES. 32

CHAPTER ONE

WHO ARE THE SHASTA?

The territory of the Shasta nation included large parts of what are today Jackson County, Oregon, and Siskiyou County, California. Ancient homes of the Shasta people stood where many modern towns can be found. The main body of the Shasta nation was divided into groups that lived in the Klamath, Scott, and Shasta River valleys.

Several peoples that lived close to the main Shasta group spoke similar languages and had a similar way of life. These nations included the Konomihu, the Okwanuchu, and the New River Shasta. Because the mountains made it difficult for people to travel from one valley to another, the Shasta people also used group names that identified their home valleys. They shared similar languages and ways of doing things, but they did not have a name for this larger group. Today, the name "Shasta" is used for all these peoples.

Mount Shasta, pictured here, may have been named for the Shasta nation. No one is certain where the word "Shasta" came from. The Native Americans we call the Shasta did not use the term to identify themselves until recent times.

CHAPTER TWO

LIVING OFF THE LAND

The Shasta people lived in a mountainous region that supported all the resources they needed to survive. The forests were home to elk, deer, and coyotes. The lakes and streams had many fish, including salmon and trout. The Shasta also had dogs that helped them hunt.

While they were hunting, Shasta men had to follow many religious rules. The rules showed respect for the animals they hunted and the natural world.

The plant life of the Shasta region was also very rich. The hills had pine and oak forests. The nuts from these trees were important food sources. There were also manzanita berries, wild plums, wild grapes, and plants with tasty seeds or roots.

The Shasta people didn't have farms. Instead, they encouraged the growth of certain kinds of plants by setting fires to burn away unwanted plants. The burnt land allowed wanted plants to move in and grow. The Shasta people also spread seeds to increase the amount of the plants they liked or needed.

CHAPTER THREE

WHAT THEY ATE

Shasta women sometimes used large, flat rocks and **cylinder**-shaped stones called pestles to grind nuts into flour. When these tools were used together with a special kind of basket, they were called a hopper mortar. Hopper mortars were also used to grind dried fish, fish bones, and dried meat into powder, which could be mixed with water to create an **edible** paste.

Shasta cooks also toasted insects, such as crickets and grasshoppers. Manzanita berries were mixed with water to make a cider-like drink.

Some Shasta cooks used earthen ovens or pits to roast food. They'd dig a hole, build a fire inside, and allow it to burn for hours. Food was wrapped in leaves and placed in the hole after the hot embers were removed. Dirt or rocks were then piled on top of the food. A few hours later, the roasted bundles could be dug up.

Acorns were an important resource for the Shasta. They ground acorns into powder and soaked it in water to get rid of the natural poisons it contained.

CHAPTER FOUR

WHERE THEY LIVED

Most of the Shasta people used two kinds of houses. During the winter, each family built a rectangular home called an *umma*. The walls and roof were created using dirt and wood. An *umma* was built inside a pit that measured between 3 and 6 feet (0.9 and 1.8 m) deep. The roof had a small opening that allowed smoke to escape and made it possible for sunlight to enter the room. The entrances to the houses usually faced the water. A single opening was created at one end and a door was made from hide or reeds.

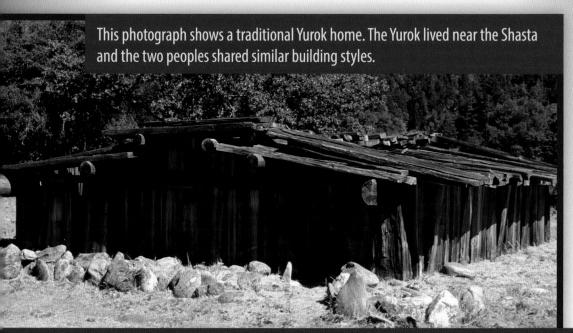

This photograph shows a traditional Yurok home. The Yurok lived near the Shasta and the two peoples shared similar building styles.

Reeds are tall, grasslike plants that grow in or near water. The Shasta people used reeds to build their homes and make tools.

During spring, most Shasta people moved into villages in the high country for the warmer seasons. Their temporary mountain homes were brush or bark huts. Older people and individuals who weren't strong enough to climb into the mountainous places stayed in the main villages.

Most of the summer houses were round and measured less than 10 feet (3 m) across. These houses were shaped like small domes or cones. In the Shasta Valley, the people lived in larger cone-shaped houses that were similar to their winter homes. Several families would share one large structure. The furniture in the houses included wooden stools, reed mats, and bundles of reeds that served as a carpet.

In some of the Shasta territory, pine needles replaced reeds as floor coverings and beds. Bed sheets and covers were made from reeds and animal skins. The cooking tools were kept in two areas near the door. The walls were lined with the family possessions. Much of the space was taken up by storage baskets and reed sacks that were filled with dried fish, dried meat, and edible plants that had been ground into flour.

Shasta Valley is located in modern-day Northern California.

CHAPTER FIVE

SOCIAL STRUCTURE

The Shasta people's smallest social group was the family. If a man wanted to get married, he had to give his future wife's family a certain amount of money. People from the same village usually didn't get married. An unmarried couple often moved in with the future husband's relatives. When a man died, his oldest brother or son gained the right to use his fishing or hunting areas.

One or more families formed a village. Village leaders included chiefs and the older people, who formed a council of **advisors**. The Shasta people also had a number of doctors and religious leaders. These groups owned sacred objects that were thought to hold special powers. The doctors and religious leaders were treated with respect. Sometimes, people feared them because they thought the doctors would use their powers to hurt them. Most of the doctors were women.

Some Shasta villages had sweathouses like the one pictured here, which was built by the Hupa Indians. Only men were allowed in sweathouses, where a small fire was kept glowing at the center of the room. When they decided to have a sweat bath, fuel was added to the fire, and the room was filled with hot air and smoke.

CHAPTER SIX

GOVERNMENT

The people of each village owed their loyalty to their village chief, who **inherited** his position from his father or brother.

The people of a village had to give special gifts of food and other things to their chief. Chiefs were responsible for settling disagreements between villagers. If someone committed a crime, the chief would often arrange for the person to pay a fine to the person they'd wronged. If the criminal couldn't pay, the chief used his own money. Chiefs also shared their food and other belongings when there were shortages. Every chief gave speeches telling his followers to be kind, to keep the peace, and to work hard. A chief's wife often gave speeches to the women of the community.

In addition to village chiefs, there was a chief for each of the four major divisions of the Shasta people.

On special occasions, such as ceremonies, community leaders wore feather collars and headdresses. Many of these coverings were made with brightly colored woodpecker feathers.

CHAPTER SEVEN

RELIGION

Through religion and doing the right thing, Shasta people worked hard to balance the forces in the world that surrounded them. The Shasta elders taught the young people many different religious stories. The stories were told over and over again for centuries with very few changes.

Religious celebrations marked each stage of a person's life. There were special prayers and dances for marriages and births and for when a person took on special responsibilities as a leader, warrior, or doctor. When a boy became 13 years old, he was expected to go off into the high mountains in search of a vision, or special dream, that would improve his ability to hunt, fish, or gamble. Some men repeated this journey several times during their lives. When a girl turned 13, she spent time away from her village. During this time she was taught special **rituals**.

Ritual dances took place to music that was performed using hide drums, rattles made from deer hooves, and bone and wood flutes.

CHAPTER EIGHT

TRADE

The Shasta people traded resources and goods within their territory. When a group from one valley went to visit another, they often brought food, which was exchanged for local products. The Shasta also went on trips to neighboring villages to gamble. Shasta people often used shell beads as money. Almost everything was assigned a certain number of beads.

A number of things were traded with outside groups. The Shasta traded baskets with their neighbors. Salt, seaweed, shells, beads, and otter skins were gathered by people who lived along the coast. **Obsidian**, which was used to make sharp chipped-stone tools, was obtained from the neighboring Achumawi people. Canoes and pine nut necklaces were created by the Wintu, who lived south of the Shasta.

The Shasta people usually tried to avoid wars. However, fights did sometimes break out between Shasta villages and their trading neighbors.

The shell of the olive snail was used to make beads commonly traded between the American Indian nations of the California region.

CHAPTER NINE

WARFARE

The Shasta peoples sometimes fought wars with their neighbors, including the Modoc and the Wintu. There were also conflicts within the Shasta nation. The Shasta Valley and Scott Valley groups sometimes fought each other, and there were also conflicts between the Klamath River Shasta and the Kammatwa.

The main Shasta weapons were bows and arrows and spears. Much of the fighting took place at night. In order to protect themselves in combat, some of the warriors wore a kind of armor made from elk hide and wooden rods. The rods, made of split branches, were held together by **hemp** cords. Many men also wore a protective headband of hide, like a helmet. Shasta warriors often wore war paint, covering their faces and their skin with painted spots. These helped identify friends and acted as religious symbols, which they believed would protect them.

This painting, made in 1846, illustrates a meeting of American soldiers discussing the U.S. president's orders to invade California, which was then part of Mexico. Two American Indian men watch the meeting.

CHAPTER TEN

SPANISH ARRIVAL

In 1542, the first Spanish explorers reached what's now California. During the 200 years that followed, there were many other European visitors. However, none of these explorers and settlers reached the interior of Northern California where the Shasta people made their homes. Although the Shasta people never saw the foreigners, they did suffer many problems as a result of their arrival. The Europeans brought terrible diseases that spread across American Indian nations and killed thousands of people. It's likely that many of the Shasta people died during this era.

Between 1769 and 1850, Spaniards, Mexicans, Russians, and Americans each claimed control of the land that would become California. Although colonists of these nations lived in the California area during this time, the Shasta people lived in a region that these foreigners rarely visited.

The Spanish established missions in California like the one pictured here. The missions were communities created to spread the newcomers' religion to the American Indians.

CHAPTER ELEVEN

A CHANGING WORLD

Fur trappers from Europe and the United States were the first outsiders to wander through the Shasta territory. Between 1820 and 1846, they passed through the area during their search for beavers and other animals whose **pelts** they could sell in Asia and Europe. The foreigners came from settlements on the coast near modern Washington and Oregon.

During this period, an **epidemic** broke out among the Shasta people. The illness may have been malaria, a kind of disease spread by mosquitoes and introduced to North America by the Europeans. So many people died between 1830 and 1833 that the Shasta leaders tried to block the entrance of any nonnative person into their communities.

By 1846, however, some of the outsiders' trade goods, such as iron tools, were becoming important to the Shasta people. This lead to increased contact with Europeans.

Hunters in California traded furs from animals such as beavers, sea otters, seals, and weasels. This photo shows a beaver pelt being stretched and dried.

CHAPTER TWELVE

THE SHASTA AND THE UNITED STATES

In 1848, the discovery of gold in California's Sierra Nevada brought large numbers of newcomers into the Shasta world. The arrival of the miners started an era of suffering for the Shasta people. When white people arrived, they simply took over the Shasta's land. Judges and courts encouraged the newcomers to enslave American Indian children. Most miners believed that all American Indians should be killed, sent to some other place, or forced to change lifestyles to be more like Europeans.

In 1851, some of the Shasta people made a treaty with the United States. The Shasta were to be given part of Scott Valley in exchange for giving up their claim to the rest of their homeland. The United States government promised to stop the miners from attacking their villages. Unfortunately, the U.S. Congress refused to **ratify** the treaty.

The miners who flooded into California during the gold rush were called the forty-niners. This photo shows a forty-niner looking for gold in 1850.

CHAPTER THIRTEEN

THE SHASTA TODAY

Between 1853 and 1856, the Shasta people fought the Rogue River Wars against U.S. soldiers and miners who attacked them. A treaty at the end of the first war led to the establishment of the Rogue River **reservation**. However, the Shasta people were still attacked by white miners and a second war began in 1855. In 1856, the Rogue River reservation was closed. The Shasta survivors were forced to march to a reservation at Grande Ronde in Oregon. Later, they were forced to Fort Hoskins in Oregon.

By 1910, the Shasta population, which once numbered about 6,000 people, had fewer than 120 survivors. In 1958, the last two Shasta reservations in California were **eliminated**.

The U.S. government no longer recognizes the Shasta as a legal American Indian nation. Today, many surviving Shasta people still disagree with this decision and continue to fight for their rights.

GLOSSARY

advisor (add-VY-zuhr) Someone who helps others make decisions.

cylinder (SIH-luhn-duhr) A solid object with straight parallel sides and two circular ends shaped like a tube.

edible (EH-duh-bull) Safe to eat.

eliminate (ih-LIH-muh-nayt) To do away with something.

epidemic (eh-puh-DEH-mik) A sickness that spreads widely and affects many people at once.

hemp (HEMP) A plant used to make rope and fabric.

inherit (ihn-HEHR-uht) To get something, such as a title, after a person in your family dies.

obsidian (uhb-SIH-dee-uhn) A black, glassy rock formed by quickly cooling lava.

pelt (PELT) A usually undressed skin with its hair, wool, or fur.

ratify (RAA-tuh-fy) To formally approve.

reservation (reh-zuhr-VAY-shun) Land set aside by the government for specific American Indian nations to live on.

ritual (RIH-choo-ull) A religious ceremony, especially one consisting of a series of actions performed in a certain order.

INDEX

A
Achumawi, 20
Asia, 26

C
California, 4
chiefs, 14, 16

E
Europe, 26
Europeans, 24, 26, 28

G
Grande Ronde, 30

H
hopper mortar, 8
Hoskins, Fort, 30
Hupa, 14

J
Jackson County, 4

K
Kammatwa, 22
Klamath River, 4, 22
Konomihu, 4

M
Mexicans, 24
Mexico, 22
missions, 24
Modoc, 22

N
New River Shasta, 4

O
Okwanuchu, 4
Oregon, 4, 30

R
reservation, 30
Rogue River Wars, 30
Russians, 24

S
Scott River, 4
Scott Valley, 22, 28
Shasta, Mount, 4
Shasta River, 4
Shasta Valley, 12, 22
Sierra Nevada, 28
Siskiyou County, 4
Spaniards, 24
sweathouse, 14

U
umma, 10

V
villages, 11, 14, 16, 18, 20, 28

W
Washington, 26
Wintu, 20, 22

Y
Yurok, 10

PRIMARY SOURCE LIST

Page 15
Hupa sweathouse. Photograph. 1923. Now kept at the Library of Congress Prints and Photographs Division Washington, D.C.

Page 25
Mission San José. Photograph. Alameda County California ca. 1866. San Francisco: Thomas Houseworth & Co. Now kept at the Library of Congress Prints and Photographs Division Washington, D.C.

Page 29
A forty-niner peers into the silt of California's American River. Photograph. By L. C. McClure. 1850. From *History of the United States*, Viking Penguin, New York, 1998.

WEBSITES

Due to the changing nature of Internet links, PowerKids Press has developed an online list of websites related to the subject of this book. This site is updated regularly. Please use this link to access the list: www.powerkidslinks.com/saic/shas